Sacred Scar

Poems

Sacred Scar

Poems

Scott Hales

GREG KOFFORD BOOKS
SALT LAKE CITY

ISBN: 978-1-58958-836-3 (paperback)
Also available in ebook.

Greg Kofford Books
P. O. Box 1362
Draper, UT 84020
www.gregkofford.com
facebook.com/gkbooks
twitter.com/gkbooks

Library of Congress Control Number: 2025950685

For Lydia

Contents

"I said to myself, the essence of every faith consists in its giving life a meaning which death does not destroy."

Leo Tolstoy, *A Confession*

Compilation

When faith snaps at my neck
like a mousetrap, I refuse to learn
my lesson. I take the risk
and return for the cheese.

Once, while praying
late at night,
I told God I hated him,
and I meant it too.
The next day I was back
in his service, committed.

What is sainthood, after all,
but suffering and mad devotion
canonized?

I want to die believing
I will rise again with you.

the boy, his burden

Stigmata

When I think of the five wounds
of Christ, I think of you, St. Francis,
kneeling in ecstasy on La Verna,
your palms open, ready to receive
the stigmata from the little seraph
on the cross. And I think too of the time
I swept up trash in Brazil, and my own
soft palms, naked against the broom's
coarse grain, blistered both and burst,
blessing me with my own red set of sores,
identical to yours. For a week or so,
everyone wanted, like Thomas, to see
my hands, to touch the tender, angry marks.
Was that how it was for you, day
after day, your raw wounds weeping,
festering for guests, miracles on display?
My wounds eventually went away.
Later, when my children were small,
we would wave to a wooden statue of you
on our way to church. You stood erect,
hands out, your arms and shoulders
covered in a congregation of birds,
as you preached a silent sermon
to the wolves in the street. My kids
are older now, and we've moved away,
but they still talk about you as if you were
a favorite uncle or a long-lost friend—
a sacred scar of memory, slow to mend.

Classroom Management

Whenever I long to see chalk dust
on my shoes or have lesson plans
again in my head, I remember Saint Cassian
of Imola, the Roman schoolteacher
so smitten with the Good News of Christ
that he refused to pray to pagan gods,
not even to get tenure. Unimpressed,
the emperor or department chair—
I can't remember who—tied him
to a tether ball post in the middle
of the playground and sentenced him
to death by students. And how
the students came, slates and iron styli
in hand, ready to turn these tools lethal,
to slay the pious pedant who slapped
their hands and swatted their rumps
for failing tests and chewing bubble gum
in class. Later, the kids said it was a joy
to slay him so slowly, one small stab
of the styli or slap of the slate at a time.
Ready to die a martyr's death, he urged
them all to hurry. But still they delayed,
disobedient to the end, consulting
scrawled anatomy notes to avoid
piercing major arteries or slashing
vital organs. It made him proud
to see them apply his lessons so.
Before they dealt the killing blow,
he gave them all top marks.

St. Patrick Spends His Big Day at My House

His morning begins with Lucky Charms
in milk dyed green with food coloring,
but rather than eat only the marshmallows,
like everyone else, he savors each bite,
even after the whole grain shapes get soggy
and swell to twice their size. He then dresses
in his saintly vestments, making sure to wear
his green chasuble so no one pinches him
as he stands beside the front door and hands
us each our lunches as we leave for school
and work. As a guest, he has nowhere else
to be but here, so he stretches out on the couch
and watches *The Quiet Man, Darby O'Gill
and the Little People,* and half of Lindsay Lohan's
Irish Wish before television loses its novelty
and he steps outside to pick a shamrock
bouquet and banish snakes from my yard.
By the time he's done, my wife and kids
are home, so he helps them hang green
and yellow streamers above the dinner table
while corned beef simmers in the slow cooker
and Irish soda bread bakes in the oven.
At half past five, I arrive in my green Subaru,
my pockets full of chocolate doubloons
I filched from a pot at the end of the rainbow,
and we sit down with Patrick at the head
of the table, where he invokes the Holy Trinity
and blesses our meal. Later, he and I sneak off
to the Olive Garden bar, the closest thing
we have to a local pub, and he orders a pint
of Guinness while I, a Mormon, drink Sprite.
And there we sit, two pals on the luckiest day

of the year, swapping tales of Irish pirates
and twenty-first century life as sleepy-eyed
suburbanites slurp down bowls of never-ending
pasta and listen to the silvery-smooth sound
of Dean Martin crooning about amore.

Restlessness on the Flight

You can only dream so much
of angels and admonitions
before sleep becomes a terror
you long to escape.
A craftsman from Nazareth,
Joseph never expected a life
on the road, hiding from tyrants
and swords in the shadow
of a pyramid. At night, no matter
where he lies, he hears the Nile
crawling steadily through the sand
and feels the pulsing rhythm
of his heart pounding in his ear
like the tramping feet of soldiers in pursuit.

Second Grief

Without ceremony, soldiers strip his body
from the cross and dump it on a heap
of other broken corpses waiting to be burned.
It's here, at this place of skulls,
that Mary, his mother, claims his remains
and asks the man from Arimathea to bear
them to the sepulcher. Her sorrow is heavy,
like a hundred wet river stones.
                              Later, as she wraps
her son in a shroud, she remembers nights in Bethlehem
when she swaddled him beneath a comet's glow
and sang half-remembered psalms of David,
the poet-king. There among the cattle and sheep,
she thought she knew what lay ahead. But now,
as she covers his face, she wonders how much
she ever understood. Three decades is enough
to erode the memory of an angel's voice. And she
was so young then. She grieved over Gabriel's words,
that much she remembers. They sat like stray embers
on her heart. But this second grief burns wildly,
like a lightning-struck field, and all she wants
to know is if his end, there on the cross,
his body on display, lacerated and humiliated,
pinned between thieves, was really what his father
had in mind so long ago. Or had she messed up
somewhere along the way, sending her son down
a more brutal path?
                              Tonight, there is room
at the inn where Mary stays. And as she climbs
to the spot where Jesus last broke bread, she thinks
once more about his birth, how he whimpered

and then cried so loud she thought she'd hurt him.
When he finally took to her breast, his first act of grace,
she cried too. He was going to be all right,
this little king without a crown, perfect in her arms.

Saint Joan

for Emily

While you watch
Dance Moms, I think
about the tortured eyes
of Maria Falconetti
in *The Passion of Joan of Arc*
and how she, as Joan,
who was your age
at the siege of Orléans,
suffered, like Christ,
on the bread of sorrow
and the water of affliction
to take her place at the top
of God's pyramid.
I think too
of the fiendish acrobats
and contortionists
who mugged for the camera
with feral delight,
wrangling their bodies
into hellish shapes
while the jailer snipped away
at Joan's close-cropped hair
until all that remained
was her ravaged scalp
and tears like great drops
of blood tumbling
down her cheeks.

Christopher

Reprobus, the dog-headed giant—
toe to crown, more than seven feet tall—
plods across the river with a burden
on his broad back: an infant in tiny robes
and a golden halo behind his ears.
He is heavy as lead, this child,
and only getting heavier as the water
rises. Not long ago, Reprobus and his fists
bore the chain of a goat-legged king
with eyes like the morning star and hair
the color of campfire before dawn.
Every day was money and blood,
blood and money—knocking heads
and breaking bones in sordid cities
somewhere east of Antioch. But he gave
that life up for the boy, his burden,
whom even the goat king feared—
this child climbing higher and higher,
from back to shoulders, from shoulders
to neck, each step a weight, pushing
him deeper into the rising river.
With no one looking, Reprobus knows
he can cast the child off, like a cross,
to keep from drowning. He has killed
others before, and no one cared.
But he made a promise at the riverbank
to this boy with wounded hands
and bleeding pores, this burden he bears,
even now, as it takes his battered life,
as he always knew it would.

Saint Melor

Melor, the little boy with a silver hand
and a bronze foot, stands in the sanctuary,
a pious cyborg of sorts, an object of pity
and adoration. He reminds me of you,
with his yellow hair and blue eyes.
You used to hold toy cars as tenderly
as he holds that stiff severed hand,
but I have never seen such a saintly look
of suffering on your face, not once.
Last summer, when you fell off your bike
and ran inside, sobbing, your palms
pebble-torn, I sat you by the sink,
turned on the faucet, and scrubbed
your hands clean while you screamed
in my ear and made a face so wretched
I thought Legion had wrung out your soul.
After his father's death, Prince Melor
nearly lost his life to a throne-hungry uncle.
But the man was not unreasonable,
like so many of his kind, and the boy
limped away from the executioner's blade
with his life and two fewer limbs.
If you want to know, this story, like life,
ends with death for everyone.
But not before the prince's prosthetic hand
begins to writhe like a moonlit spider
caught in its own crystal web: a miracle
for the boy with the suffering face
and a neck now cocked for the martyr's block.

Ferryman Lee

Cast off, banished
to the edge
of a red rock hell,
he seeks redemption
without penance,
a real-life Julian,
the imaginary saint
who murdered
his parents
while they slept in his bed.

Flight

In paintings, Joseph of Cupertino,
    the flying friar, the slack-jawed saint,
      spreads his arms majestically,

his hands and fingers like feathers
    as he floats above an astonished crowd.
      Levitating beside a window or a cross,

he looks like a basketball player
    going in for the dunk on the cover
      of *Sports Illustrated for Monks*. As a boy,

he was good for nothing, a dullard
    prone to fits of anger and ecstasy—
      no one you would want to see

about town or behind the altar
    at church. And for this, they hid him away.
      But God loves his underdogs

and gives them grace to fly.
    When I became a priest, someone—
      I don't know who or why—raised a hand

in opposition, and I've carried that
    ever since, like an old fob on a keychain,
      scratched and half forgotten, but still there.

If I have one regret about that day,
    it's that I did not spread my arms,
      there at the pulpit, and leap above the crowd.

the ranks of ghosts

Third Witness

We stand together at sunrise, Brother Martin,
me and your monument. It reaches out,
a granite giant screaming your name
across an empty valley. When you died,
sixteen teams of wagons, *well filled*,
climbed this rise to bury your bones.
Clarkston was no city on a hill, but the folks here
did their duty, kissing your boot-leather face goodbye
with burning coals on their lips and your witness
like evening frogsong in their ears.

You said you saw an angel in the woods,
and they believed you. Other times, your words
ran fast, like rivers after rain, toppling mountains,
spilling over valleys, flooding fields.
Like every Adam's son, you were imperfect.
Jesus called you *wicked*, and we let you bear
that cross even now, here on this Golgotha,
this crumbling stage with concrete steps
and aluminum seats. This is your life, brother.
How long has it been?

When Oliver Cowdery stepped across the veil,
he waited decades beside a wheel-rutted road.
Then Emma came, Charon-like, to pick him up
in a sturdy carriage. At first, they traveled in silence,
neither one eager to reach deep into the hornet's nest
of the past. But Emma, her hands loose on the reins,
soon spoke of the house in Harmony, where she
and Joseph and Oliver sat together each evening
by the blackened hearth, their faces dancing red
with firelight and shadow, as she led them in song.
So they traveled, those two, side by side

with memory, until they came to the Missouri River,
its eastern bank a snarl of stones and roots.
"You know, we did all right," Emma told Oliver.
"When you cross the river, you'll see."
And there she left him, waist-deep
in the water, ready to swim.

Brother Martin, wicked man, who came for you?
Or are you still waiting at the roadside?
Your body rests today beyond the glow
of traffic lights, and, if I'm being honest,
this town seems too small for you.
But how great it must be to be remembered.
We all want to see an angel, to witness to the world.
You did both. If you're still waiting, wait for me.

Big City Prophet

New York City, 1832

The boarders at the Pearl Street House
number maybe one hundred, and talking
with them at table, you'd never know
the cholera had cut its way through the city
some three months back,
and the buildings reach like Babel's tower
above the trees, but they are great
and wonderful and pleasing to God,
the maker of all things, who even now smiles
on every invention geared to making man
comfortable and wise. Yet, the people,
cast from His own iron mold, wear corruption
on their faces, and not even their silk cravats,
tall hats, and hillocks of curls can mask
their iniquity, their readiness for fire unquenchable,
His inevitable sparks.
Yes, my one true and living friend, this city,
our industrial Nineveh, has its limits, but how
the heart yearns to redeem it with a word,
to cry out, to carry its two hundred thousand souls
beyond the strangle of warehouse dust
and factory smoke. And how you rush
upon my mind like a calming flood, dear one.
If I ever find my way home,
may we seek a brighter world together.

Joseph Standing's Gun

Whitfield County, Georgia, 1879

Let's pretend you never had a gun
that summer morning in Georgia.

What was it like, in the frantic flurry
before you died, to pantomime a pistol
and shout "surrender" with all the bravado
of a boy playing sheriff?

You must have remembered
how you scattered red-cheeked chums
with that word, spoken deeply,
a voice like your father's, when chores
were done, and you had hours to play
before your mothers called you home.

Your hands were all the arms
you needed to tame a lawless town—
two hands, one magic word, and the boys
would throw their own hands high
and drop their sacks of stolen loot
in deference to your tiny tin star.

I've seen your photograph, Joseph.
You were not much older than a boy
when they shot you point-blank in the face.
You had the wavy hair and earnest eyes
of every backyard cop I've ever known.

How could you not expect the world
to stop at your command?

Portrait of a Lady without Hands:
A Postmortem

Spanish Fork, 1899

Lying there, she looks alive, caught
mid-blink or contentedly asleep.
All we have to do is tug at her puffy sleeve
and whisper her awake. She's rehearsing
for the resurrection, this Lazarus woman,

calling to our inner Christ with her lifelike
look of repose. Her raven hair is perfect—
curled tight and parted down the middle—
not quite the wispy conch of a Gibson Girl,
but something like it. And her short jacket

and lacy scarf, what we see of them, are as neat
as grief allows. So too are the white sheets,
still creased, her father hangs behind her head
while the hometown photographer unpacks
his boxy wooden camera and points it

at her face. But to us, eying her now,
these quaint respects seem immaterial
alongside the enigma of her empty sleeves.
Her eyes and mouth are so serene—
it feels impertinent to ask, even silently,

about the missing hands. And yet,
that's what we do, anticipating a tale,
some disfiguring slip of the Industrial Age.
Never mind the obvious: her hands are still there,
hidden beneath the folds of her blouse,

as easily retrieved as two dusty candlesticks
from the topmost cupboard shelf. Yes,
that's the message of this portrait: spirit
and body, not light and emulsion, are her soul.
Death and time cannot erase her.

At Cold Harbor

This evening, as I run along this sandy trail,
squirrels scamper like ghosts across dead leaves
before leaping to some nearby tree trunk
and skittering into silence. Although death
and misery appear far away, I feel them close,
crouching like the men who gouged this land
with metal tools long since rusted into dust.
Beneath this wooden bridge, blood pooled
like creek water at a dam, and soldiers, rushing,
splashed about, each side determined to wade
in their shared gore. Some of them would live
to see great wars poured out upon all nations,
minor variations on the same old theme. Others,
with bloated faces turned toward the sun,
would molder in the dried mud, week after week,
until all that remained for the northern cameras
were sun-bleached skulls and one stray boot.
My time is short, but I stop whenever I see
the soft impressions of their trenches. Here,
lice-bitten and afraid, they waited out the day,
their backs to the mud and rotting planks,
listening to artillery streak the sky like birds
of prey. Once, on Christmas Day, God wept
apocalyptic tears and spoke about this fierce
and vivid lightning, sparking retribution
from his hard, unsparing hand. For a moment,
I want to feel the fulfillment of those words,
and so I leap into a weedy scar and watch
the ranks of ghosts advance through time,
their blistered feet translucent in the setting sun.

Pioneer Ascension

Cedar Fort, 1874

When the Storm God shut the eyes
of Lucy Bailey White, he carried her
spirit to the top of Floyd's Peak
to show her the work of his hands.
She was not yet young again, but her knees
and ankles were nimble now, free
from the burden of flesh that ground
them down for over eighty years.
She leaped from crag to crag, following
the Storm God as his long hair
and electric cloak shed flakes of snow
across his path. When he stretched his arms
wide as eternity, noting this stray cow
or that irrigation ditch, Lucy saw them all
up close, as if she too carried a Divine Eye
like a telescope around her neck.
From that height, the people in town,
out for her wake, looked no taller
than stitches in a hemline. They stood
by her coffin, heads bowed, glancing
now and then at her toothless grin,
sewn shut and all but lost behind her veil.
Lucy wanted to laugh, but the Storm God
waved his hand, and the coffin closed.
Then he set a fiery coal upon her feet,
and together they soared above the valley
as every cloud from Lehi to Santaquin
converged over the mountain and spat
ice crystals and cold rain on the mourners,

refreshing their cisterns and dry wells.
And Lucy became light, her spirit one
with the Storm God as they climbed
higher and higher above the tempest.

The Great Mystery;
or, Isabelle Berry on the Eve of Her Demise

Along Short Creek, 1866

With each rising and setting sun,
Isabelle watches this weird red land catch fire,
but because bereavement and grief
have rubbed her heart raw, she perceives
the passing world around her wagon—
the wind-carved rocks and scrubby trees—
as vague shapes and interruptions.
And now that it's evening, she waits,
listening for the next world to awake,
not because night sounds comfort her,
but because she needs to know when to hold
her hands tight against her ears and pray
that coyotes and catamounts and vermin
with tiny claws and teeth stay far away.
For she has not slept since Robert, her husband,
buried their baby in Kanarraville, a betrayal
that troubles her barely literate mind
and casts arching shadows over everything
she once knew about God's kingdom
and its mysteries. For why would God
take such pains to fashion a life
after His own existence
only to snatch it away like a coin
in a magician's trick? Isabelle's own mother
bore twelve children in a wilderness
of diphtheria and death, and not one has passed.
So Isabelle has to ask: if God chooses
who lives and dies, what does that say
about Him and those who call him Father?
Tomorrow, she and Robert will die violently

on a red knoll that bears their name today
like a curse. But Isabelle does not know that yet,
not as she lies here, confused and afraid,
angry as the devilish glow of campfire on her face.
She wants to run from the future, not because
of what will happen, but because of what could.
She knows God, the Great Mystery, sees all,
watches this combustible landscape
and everything beyond it, not as gnarled shapes
or flickering shadows, but as adolescent forms,
gods in concept, sprouting into things
both terrible and sublime. And this heavy truth
presses Isabelle deep into the stony earth.
She feels it sharp against her wretched skin,
but she is too tired and stricken to scream.

For Samuel D. White, Pioneer

God's nomad, you wore out wagons
and leather for visions of better worlds—
you, the Sunday school hero
of a thousand faces, the trailblazer,
the darling of the D. U. P.
Your kind beat the devil back
to hell and pitched tents outside
its gates, and for that we crown you
kings and queens—you, our builders,
our titans who wore your prejudice
and fear like bone-white handkerchiefs
speckled with blood, your kindness
and cruelty like rings.
                    Once you wended west,
you never stopped until the grave,
and even now you live, your faces
like flint and tumbleweed, your eyes
fixed forward, hollow and cold,
a trick of light on silver and tin.
You always ask what we did
with your dreams, those roots
you planted on land that wasn't yours
to take or even God's to give,
not then.
                    And I am silent, unsure
what to say, thinking maybe
all big dreams are selfish,
all mythologies stained by tooth
and claw. But I get the yearning
to believe, to strive for brighter worlds,
to dig foundations and set stone
on stone. I too long to be God's nomad,
to wear the crown and break it too.

Local and Other Matters;
or, The Accidental Killing of Mrs. Sally W. Phelps

> God is his own interpreter
> And he will make it plain.
> —William Cowper

Sally's husband saw signs
in cosmic clutter,
so why shouldn't she?
The bridge, the ditch, the bucket,
the city, the sash—
these convergences
were with her in the womb.
So too were the Prophet's words:
how she, like the three disciples
and John, would never taste death.
All her life, she had sung
about God's mysterious ways,
and she trusted in his never-failing skill.
So when a canyon wind
assaulted the city,
snatching skylights and shingles
like martial trophies from a foe,
she shut her mouth,
toothless from old age and exhaustion,
and bared her neck
to frowning Providence
and His sovereign will.

Resurrection Prayer

Turn my bones over
with Zeke Johnson's plow.
Cut the earth. Let it bleed

into my dried veins. I offer
my thin skin willingly, Lord,
to your magical needle

and thread. Stitch each flap
of flesh together. Grease
my joints. Socket my hips.

Add organs and muscles, Lord,
sinews and sweat. Print fingertips
and freckles. Polish my well-worn

teeth. Then plant hair
like prairie grass on my head
and in my ears. I want those

who love me to know me.
Gather them together, Lord,
as soon as you can.

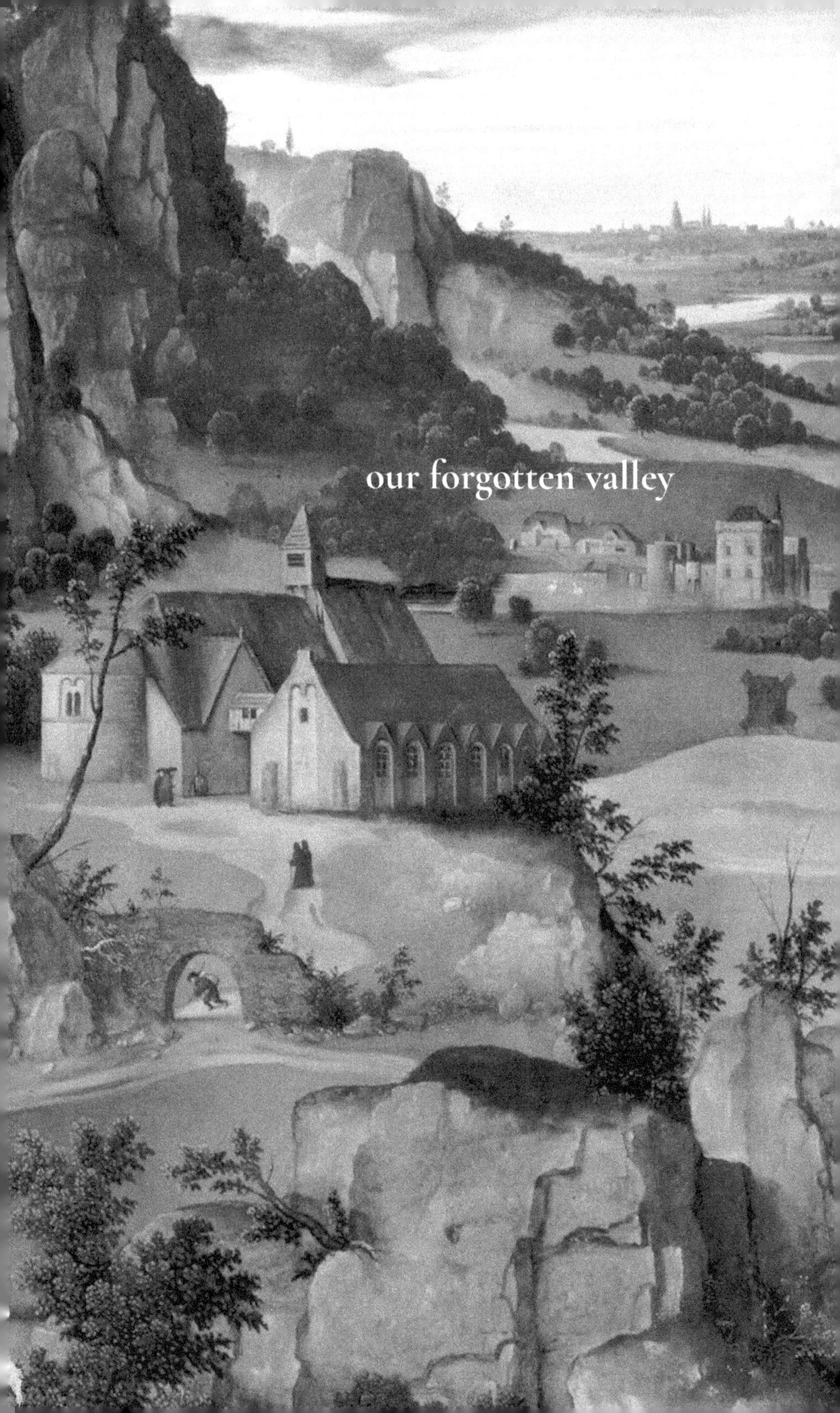
our forgotten valley

Familiar Forms

One evening, millennia ago,
someone stood here,

watched the sun set
behind the amber rim

of the mountains,
and marked the moment

with a scorpion. Today,
leaning on a steel fence,

we puzzle over legs
and claws—familiar forms

from an unfamiliar hand.
It's all we here can do.

View

The east windows glow
most mornings like memories
of vintage color photographs.
And so, from the back door,
Lake Mountain is a Technicolor
Sinai, the face of the Storm God
and his apocalyptic brow.
Light hangs on the landscape
like history, and the grim tale
it tells places three shallow graves
within our view—troubled earth
split open like a sore. But what
is forty years for a Storm God
with wandering children?
Those graves will soon be homes
for living bones, and the heavy
canvas curtain of time will fall
on the faraway scene of a lone man
with a shovel and a flashlight
and the three dead boys he hid
in the ground. And still, in silhouette,
the never-sleeping Storm God stands
with wounds in his sloping shoulders
and a mural of stars for his crown.

Holy Envy

Dust rides the warm breeze bareback,
whipping long wispy limbs through wide
suburban streets and weedy gardens.
From where I sit, swinging in the shade,
it looks like God's tenth plague rolling
down the mountain, a burly cloud
with nowhere to go but here. I step inside
and listen for a mighty Pentecostal rushing
of wind. Instead, I hear the low, bovine
murmur of the air conditioner. Outside,
the dust dissipates into scribbles, a shy
lover's poem. Disappointed, I climb
the steps, another tent maker on the road
to Damascus. Here I am, God. Blind me.

Pole Canyon

When Old Bishop Weeks heard
they found the brothers' mutilated bodies
in the canyon, he came running

to see his boys. But his eyes
shone dim in that milky morning light,
and when his rough boots snagged

on the sagebrush and stone, he fell
hard into the thorns, helpless
as a raven with a ravaged wing.

Later, after the men brought
the bodies back to Cedar Fort,
they tallied each wound, counting

on revenge and wondering
how the two brothers could come
to such a grisly end so close to home.

And Old Bishop Weeks, still tangled
in the weeds, rent his weathered coat:
Blind Isaac weeping for his sons.

Self Portrait at 42

Less concerned about my posture
than in years past, I saunter outside
to welcome the day and let the dog
do his business. My grandfathers
would have found a newspaper
waiting on their doorsteps when they
were my age, but all I see this morning
are a view of Flat Top Mountain
and the bicycles my children forgot
to put away. My hair is Prufrock-
thin but unruly, a graying shadow
of its former glory. I have brown eyes
and progressive lenses. If I see you
on the street, I might forget your name.
I am leaning into middle age the way
runners lean into the wind. I sense
the steady passage of time as a weariness
in my brain, if not my bones. Time
will change that. Tomorrow I begin
my forty-third year. Or does it start today?
That's my shadow there in the grass.

The Mouse I Killed

"because—because he was my foe."
—Thomas Hardy

Had you and I but met by some old
ancient wood, or even in the dusty hills
just east of here, I should not have thought twice
about your needle teeth and eyes
like drops of ink.
I should have seen you in a flash,
a blur of fur scurrying across a trail,
your tail an afterthought of earth tones,
nothing to worry about or chase after
with a carving knife.
But fate dealt us a different hand,
and the moment I heard you scratching
in my bathroom closet, nibbling on soap
like a lost and hungry child
blinded by the night, I wanted you dead.
All you wanted was a nice hole
somewhere along my baseboards,
a simple portal to a snappy room, cozy and clean
and thoroughly bourgeois, finely furnished
with an easy chair and a well-worn rug,
maybe a picture or two on the papered walls,
just like in the classic cartoons.
And isn't that what we all want in the end—
a warm, quaint place?

Transit of Mercury

Cross, quick as silver,
speedy messenger, herald
of the gods. Invisible to naked

eyes, you are a black speck
on the telescope, a seeming flaw
on the lens. But there you go,

wing-shod through the vacuum,
gravity's tether swinging you
around the sun like a yo-yo

in skillful hands. And we
on earth squint at you through
glass and mirror, waving our hands

like children on a school bus,
our hopeful smiles and runny noses
pressed tight against the windows.

St. Joseph to Sacramento

Underdressed and overconfident,
I plunge into a squally evening,
arms pumping, rock 'em sock 'em.
And right when I think Almighty God
has called it a night, Billy Ocean's
"Caribbean Queen" drops on my playlist
like a spider out for a stroll, and when
Ocean sings about painted-on jeans,
I remember one time in eastern Idaho,
half a lifetime ago, when my roommate
and I bought tight thrift-store Wranglers
and cowboy hats because our dates
to the college dance were geek magnets
who wanted Marlboro Men,
and all night we line danced and two-stepped
our own Texas nutcracker ballet
while our dates, unamused,
eyed the real cowboys in the room,
the ones smelling of leather and steel,
and wondered what else
they had to do to make amends
for their youthful sins.
And as I remember those jeans
and that night, I realize I'm running
on the old Pony Express trail,
and for that fact alone, reject all notions
of chance and coincidence.
That's when "Caribbean Queen" ends
and the theme of *Top Gun: Maverick*
slowly gains in altitude, and I turn a corner,
teeth to the icy wind, and soar.

Running through Cedar Pass at Sunrise

Seeing Flat Top Mountain
this morning, its cold peak
a paint pot of orange and rose,

I'm reminded of reading
Wordsworth as a sophomore
in eastern Idaho, when every

spontaneous overflow
of powerful two-hundred-year-old
feeling made me yearn to tear shirtless

through the wilderness
just beyond the undulating lava plain
outside the library window.

I wanted the world for my backyard,
a garden paradise where my poems
took roots and sprouted branches

with leaves so green they inspired
more poetry to spring from the earth.
And I wanted you sitting beside me

on a picnic blanket, congratulating
yourself on falling in love
with the shirtless poet whose poem

was the very tree giving us shade.
But now, as I approach a steep hill
and feel a dull ache in my right calf,

I mistake Shetland ponies for sheep
and wince at the unfamiliar warmth
of manure in the air, sure signs

our backyard goes no farther
than the vinyl fence dividing
our property from the neighbor's.

And I know my poems have never
become trees, but you do read them,
grateful for my day job and yours.

Uncanny Valley

A ghost with green eyes as round
and pale as honeydew glowers at me
from the rough shoulder of Highway 73.
The wraith is naked, but rather than feel
embarrassed for it, as I probably should,
I turn up my wheezing car heater and crank
some classic country music until all I hear
are static and slide guitar. It's night
and winter, and I'm too cold to care
about every apparition I see on the side
of the road. Once, while driving east
across the valley, I picked up a vanishing
hitchhiker who had known my great-uncle
in high school. She said he had a fine
truck and the sharpest crew cut north
of Provo. I dropped her off at the cemetery
and donated the sweater she left behind
to Deseret Industries. If you think that's bad,
you should hear about the time I hit
a revenant near Cedar Fort. But no,
I won't tell that one. Not yet. The ending
isn't great, and I forget the middle.

Homecoming

What better sight is there
than this: the rising or setting sun
in our forgotten valley?

some handmade lace

Daughter of the Pioneers

Like a lion wrangler, she pulls me
into a room furnished entirely, she claims,
with furniture made by Brigham Young.
And though my face is the picture
of skepticism, I'm wearing a mask,
so she rewards my muffled "wow"
with a satisfied smile. From there,
we charge across the hall to see shoes
so narrow they look like doll slippers,
and she tells me how her grandma
could not walk more than a mile
because of her tiny feet, and can you believe
how small the pioneers were compared
to us today, but boy could they make
things last. I nod and follow her
to another display: a century-old
wedding cake beside a case of silkworm
cocoons. Whispering, she tells
how pioneer women incubated them
in the warmth between their breasts
until the silk sacs stirred and the worms
wiggled free, and I nod again and murmur
my "wow" because I have no idea
if what she's saying is true.
So we go, room by room.
Here's a drum someone's uncle played
in the funeral procession of the Martyrs.
And that heavy flatiron there, the one
with the worn wooden handle?
It's honest-to-goodness proof
that pioneer women were just as strong
as pioneer men. Pick it up. You'll see.
She tells me about every knickknack

and broken piece of bric-a-brac
between me and the door. But the thing
she points out, again and again,
is the size of the clothes. Imagine,
she says, how odd it must have been
to be so small in such a rough-and-tumble world,
where shoes were neither left nor right—
and here, let me show you some handmade lace.

Insufferable and Armed

for Brittany

When the world we know scatters
like volcanic ash across a yellow sky,
and the brass locks we trusted
like God no longer keep us safe
at home, we might text our regret
for mocking the insufferable and armed
whose concrete bunkers and basement
arsenals now seem pretty smart
to those of us living among rats
and raccoons in post-suburban
trash heaps and blackened buses.
But we might also double down,
as losers often do, sure our gamble
with the future was not only right,
but also righteous. For who wants
to live with more fear when fear
already sits like a jangling key ring
in your pocket or some scratchy sand
in your shoe? And, let's be honest,
who wants to spend the apocalypse
munching stale granola bars
and standing guard just inside
an electric fence? Not us, surely.
Today, when we see the flags
and billboards and bumper stickers
smeared with swears and slurs,
we roll our eyes like irritated teens
and text our angst, as friends often do.
And I bet we'll act no differently in the end
as long as cell towers still stand.
For, when civilization crumbles

like day-old cake, the last thing I want
is for you to fall to zombies or nukes
or armies of armed insufferables
without first feeling the familiar buzz
of a notification on your phone
and reading a few snarky words from me.

PG-13 Horror

for Ella

Blood oozes and drips
in these movies. It never spurts
like a janky Italianate fountain
in someone's backyard.

Hot teens in tight clothes
still die every fifteen minutes
or so, but you never see them
suffer shockingly sudden deaths

on screen. The camera always
cuts away, like cheap grace,
to gnarled trees against a night sky
or to a naked yellow bulb

dangling from a black cord
somewhere else in the basement.
And always when that happens,
we lock eyes, more amused

than shocked, so assured
we are that tonight's tomorrow,
for all its mystery, will still rise
like a ghost to haunt our days

with meaning and memory.

Instant

> "Yesterday won't be over until tomorrow and
> tomorrow began ten thousand years ago."
> —William Faulkner, *Intruder in the Dust*

It is not yet two o'clock, and I want to say
the instant doesn't matter: you crouched
behind a rail fence and a furled rebel flag,
waiting for Pickett to signal the advance.
In no future does this damned gamble pay off,
poor mountain boy, even if you win the day.
But Faulkner was right: all is in the balance,
and nothing has happened yet.
                                    In this instant,
somewhere along the Federal line, a Minié ball
with your name on it, wrapped in cheap paper,
waits in a cartridge box for some Billy Yank
to send your way. And I can tell you what happens.
In another instant, you grip your musket
and charge across that field, a desperate skeleton
blind with hunger, ready to face the enemy
with one lead ball and no bayonet.
                                    Maybe
you reach the wall. Maybe you only get in range.
Either way, that Minié ball whistles a hole
through your hip.
                          Once upon a time, I wondered
what might have happened if that ball had struck
you square in the gut, somewhere soft and vital
and easy to infect, thus consigning our tomorrows
to a slow, festering death, ten thousand years

in the making. But I was missing the point
of this instant. You are in the balance, not me.
It is not yet two o'clock on this July afternoon.
Nothing has happened, and you can still walk away.

Poe

Like a bird weary of wind
and sky, you nest upon my knees.
You exhale, and your breath

sputters like the death rattle
of a rusty pressure valve.
You are chapter and verse

of canine ennui this late summer
Saturday. I am powerless
to move you. The world burns

apocalyptic red, and you act
like judgment day is optional.
If Timmy fell down a well

or came nose to nose
with a spring-loaded cougar,
you would shut your ears

against his desperate whistles
and think, "I can always find
another little farm boy."

Dentist Appointment

for Rebecca

The building squats on cracked asphalt
like a dormant cinder cone,
and when we open the glass door,
we feel the earth groan
as the stairwell sucks us in,
wrapping us in a warm, stale funk
of cigarette smoke and lemon-scented cleaner.
And we race to the upper landing,
skipping steps as we go, while our mother,
a twin on each hip, stumbles
like an unsteady memory through the door
and begins her slow climb,
her tightrope act on weary knees.
By the time she summits the steps,
we are already halfway down the hall,
tasting a fresher nicotine
and buzzing to the *musica universalis*
of the flickering fluorescent lights.
A few more feet, and we are outside
the office, panting like sprinters
on a high school track, elbows out,
sucking in toxic air as we bicker
over the shame and glory of being
"First the Worst" and "Second the Best."
On less contentious days, we might drink
from the rusty water fountain
between the restroom doors.

But today we simply push our way
into the blinding light of the office,
throw off our coats like prize fighters
in the ring, and battle it out
for the latest issue of *Highlights*.

Aftermath

for Ishmael and his family

In my post-apocalyptic fantasies,
I skip the brutal gaspunk battles, the wars
for wasteland dominance, the petty reigns
of junkyard knuckleheads and growling chieftains
with beards the size of Montana,
and I jump ahead to soft bucolic scenes
where I work a carrot patch on a communal farm
somewhere on the outskirts of a ruined city.
You are there with your family, bickering
as always, but also happy to be alive and safe
after so many decades of chaos and surrender.
At night, as we gather around our oil lamps
and homemade candles, we tell stories
for hours, variations on half-remembered movies
and young adult novels, and we laugh
and sometimes cry about the hollow world
we lost, the instantaneous connection,
the cell phones and flame wars, the rumor and news.
We know nothing now but what we know
and speak of nothing save what keeps us alive.
And when we bury our dead beyond the pasture,
we each speak a memory to ferry their worn-out souls
beyond this shattered world, and we do so
hoping that our weeping God, broken by years
of heartache and horror, has strength enough
to welcome them back, to build their mansions
in a realm of cloud, to give them rest.

Proxies

In your white jumpsuit, you look
as small as a rabbit in a pet shop,
only more excited than scared,
and when I see you standing at the edge
of the font, unsure what to do
with the locker key coiled
around your wrist, you look
every one of your eleven years
all at once, and innocence sits lightly
on your shoulder like the dove
that fluttered over Jordan
when Jesus himself was baptized,
and all I can think is how happy I am
that you are happy, that life
has not yet hurt you, that you
still have so much of life to live.
In the font, you grip my arm
while I recite the names of women
long dead, ancestors who, like you,
felt the innocence of girlhood
like a meadow, but who soon felt
each stone of mortality like a fracture
in the bone. They grew old, fell in love,
had happy days and sad, prayed,
pleaded with God and maybe sensed
a silence, dreamed and surrendered,
lived, survived, and died.
And now, as you take upon their names,
one by one, you take upon their lives,
and for a moment, buried together,
you become the same in the eyes of God,
sisters of experience and renewal,
proxies of future and past.

Cousin

I remember the afternoon
my mom sat me down
at the kitchen table
me and my other siblings
or maybe just the oldest three
and told us how a tumor in your brain
had made you blind
and how relieved I was
because your sister had just died
and blindness by comparison
did not seem so bad

I only saw you once after that
my only memory of you
and I can still see us on the floor
at grandma's house
you holding a pair of dice
and everyone thinking how great it was
because you were blind and playing
board games like a regular kid
and how we cheered you on
as you tossed the dice a little too hard
and how they skipped across the board
like two flat stones on a glassy lake
with just enough force
to fly straight at my face

You died soon after that
and late last night
when I forgot your name
I searched online for your obituary
and found a photograph of you
in a white dress

and I remembered that picture
hanging on our refrigerator
a tiny shrine to a dead blind girl
and how even though we weren't close
I claimed your tragedy as my own

This is my cousin who died
I'd tell my friends
and if they caught me crying
I'd say I was thinking about you
and sometimes I'd be telling the truth

Magic Shop

We ride the Metro downtown,
but before we tour the Washington Monument
and the National Gallery,
you take me to Al's Magic Shop
on Vermont Avenue.
And on the way you talk
about Harry Blackstone Sr.,
Melbourne Christopher,
and the other magicians you saw
when you were a boy
practicing sleight-of-hand tricks
with cards and ropes
in front of the bathroom mirror.

At the shop, I browse
beginner magic tricks and books
about Harry Houdini
while you chat with Al
and some other customers—
all old men, all strangers—
about how you and your friends
used to come to the city on the weekends
after the war, back when the shop
was still on Pennsylvania Avenue,
and how Al knew every trick in the store
and could demonstrate it too.

In the end, we don't buy anything,
but later, at the top of the Washington
Monument, we go from window
to window, and you show me
every landmark
from the Lincoln Memorial

to the DC temple, and seeing
the city spread out like a map,
with roads and treetops disappearing
at the blue-gray horizon, you recall
summer days forty years earlier
when you'd ride your bike
from Bethesda down to the capital
to fish along the Potomac
or wander the National Mall
until the sun hung low over Arlington
and it was almost too dark
to find your way home.

Easy

We never ease into our evenings
anymore, and our lounging
on the couch to watch a show
or two on television is hardly effortless.
We do not simply hang out, like Orion
in the southern sky. We collapse,
wincing and groaning, derelict cars
out for one last drive.
Everything hurts, even rest.
And life goes so fast, pinwheeling
around us in a psychedelic blur
where one color barges in
on another without apology.
More and more, we want easy.
Or we want time to matter again,
each minute more than a fleck
of black paint on a spinning clock.
Last week, I said we'd laugh
about this in fifty years, but now
I can't remember what this was.
And we don't have those fifty years.

Villanelle Set in the ER

You had the chance, and so you had to try.
I never questioned why. I knew. But still,
that room was such an ugly place to die.

Outside, a red sign flickered in the sky
to light your last hurrah. You knew the drill.
You had the chance, and so you had to try,

to swat that buzzing, interposing fly
and shush the voices in your ear. But still,
that room was such an ugly place to die,

a vapid cell, an antiseptic sty
with tiled floors and harsh fluorescent chill.
You had the chance, and so you had to try,

no matter where your body came to lie.
That night, the end was not for me. But still,
that room was such an ugly place to die.

When waltzing stars go out, we'll cease to cry.
That's what I say and maybe always will.
You had the chance, and so you had to try.
That room was such an ugly place to die.

an afterthought

Advice to a Young Mormon Poet

Just know you are not the first
to take up your pen. Our people
crossed oceans and prairies

and wrote poems along the way.
Read their letters and diaries.
You'll find poems scribbled

between lines and in margins.
And then read everything else,
not just the poems. We have lost

traditions. Find them.
Respond. React. Restore.
Do your homework. Recover

what we've forgotten as a rose
blossoming in the desert. But
don't get mired in the past.

Treat it like a storehouse stocked
with two centuries of consecrated
goods. Engage the present.

Imagine futures. If you spot Zion
in the sky, put it in your pocket
for another day. We have enough

prophets and priests. We even
have plenty of poets, so nothing
you say will be entirely new.

It all comes down to how you say it.
Don't echo the echo chamber.
Take up the divining rod. Dowse

with Oliver for something
hidden and true. Gaze with Eliza
at the glittering expanse. Follow her

into the wilderness. And, yes,
though it sounds trite, go to church.
Read your scriptures. Pray.

notes

I never know how many notes to give my readers. T. S. Eliot gave his readers plenty of notes for *The Waste Land*, but this book isn't *The Waste Land* and most people, including poetry lovers, google what's unfamiliar. So, unlike what I did in *Hemingway in Paradise and Other Mormon Poems*, I'm not going to weigh down the end of this book with a lot of trivia. If you want to know who Saint Melor is, you can pull out your smartphone and look him up. His story is fascinating and certainly fictitious. But still, what an odd little story.

I have long been interested in the lives of Catholic saints, and the poems in the first section of this book reflect that. Most of the poems are efforts to draw parallels between my experiences and theirs. The rest are efforts to understand the relationship between sainthood and suffering. In writing about these saints, I relied on the third edition of David Hugh Farmer's *The Oxford Dictionary of Saints*, which I bought at a thrift store some years ago.

Ferryman Lee is John D. Lee, one of the perpetrators of the Mountain Meadows Massacre. If you want to know more about him, you can google him. But you can also read the works of Richard E. Turley Jr. and his coauthors Ronald W. Walker, Glen M. Leonard, and Barbara Jones Brown. And the works of Juanita Brooks, of course.

The poems in the second section are Mormon history poems, including the Civil War poem "Cold Harbor." I wrote that poem as a mediation on Joseph Smith's apocalyptic

December 25, 1832, revelation on war. Perceptive readers will also recognize "Big City Prophet" as a poem based on Joseph Smith's October 13, 1832, letter to his wife, Emma.

The tragic story of Sally Waterman Phelps's death is not well known. Reports of it can be found in the January 4, 1874, issue of the *Salt Lake Herald,* the January 5, 1874, issue of the *Ogden Junction,* and the January 7, 1874, issue of the *Deseret News.*

Shortly after finishing *Hemingway in Paradise,* I wanted to write a book of poems about Utah's Cedar Valley, where I call home. That book never took shape, but I did write enough poems about the valley to fill the third section of this book.

Old Bishop Weeks in "Pole Canyon" is Allen Weeks, the first Latter-day Saint bishop of Cedar Fort, Utah. On August 8, 1854, his sons William and Warren were found "horribly mutilated" in the canyon near their home. For more information, see "Shocking Murder," *Deseret News*, August 17, 1854. Lucy Bailey White and her son Samuel D. White are my direct ancestors. Lucy, one of my few historic ties to Cedar Valley, passed away in Cedar Fort in 1874. She is buried there in an unmarked grave.

The final section is composed entirely of poems written for or about others, including the family dog. "Villanelle Set in the ER" is about the death of my sister-in-law, Lydia Unklesbay, who edited *Hemingway in Paradise* so masterfully. This book is dedicated to her. My greatest fear, I think, is being forgotten, and I have a habit of sometimes projecting my fears onto others. *Sacred Scar* is my small effort to ensure that Lydia's memory lives on.

The book's afterthought, I hope, speaks for itself.

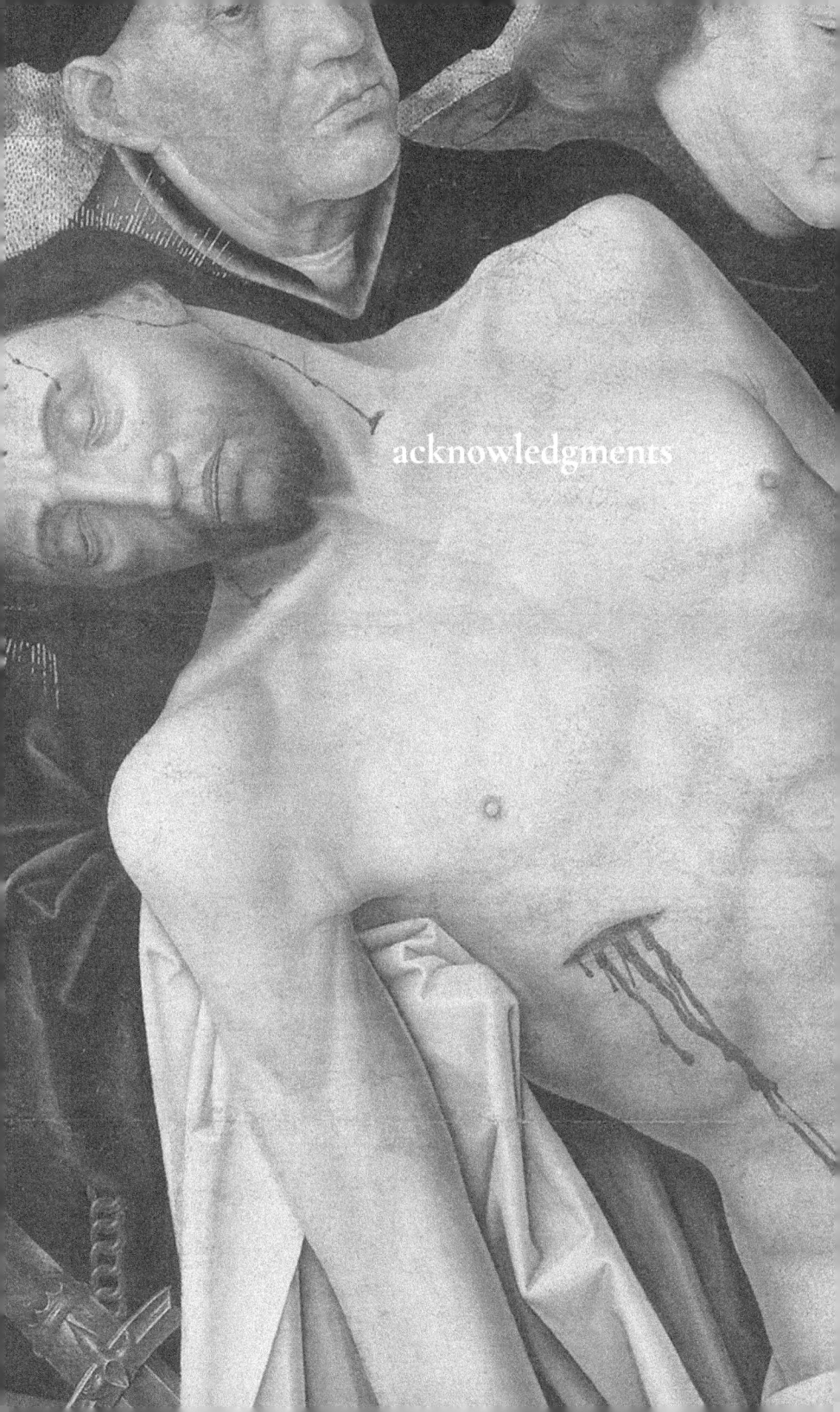

acknowledgments

This book came together by trial and error. I cobbled together an early draft in March 2024, but it lacked focus and maturity. So, I tinkered with it for about a year until I finally figured out what I wanted it to say. And once I knew what I wanted the book to be, it became easier for me to decide which poems belonged in the book and which ones did not.

I am grateful to the talented Mormon poets who gather each February to share their work in the MoPoWriMo Facebook group. They were the supportive first readers for most of the poems in this collection. I am also grateful to Kevin Klein, Merrijane Rice, Dave Nielsen, Shannon Milliman, Jared Forsyth, and Petra Javadi-Evans for reading manuscripts and offering helpful suggestions. I also owe a great deal to the members of my super chill CHD writing group for reading an earlier draft of this book and letting me know that it was OK to include some funny poems in it.

My heartfelt appreciation goes out to the editors of the journals that first published the following poems (or earlier versions of them):

Bleating Thing Magazine: "Aftermath"
Dappled Things: "Classroom Management" and "Stigmata"
Inscape: "Portrait of a Lady without Hands: A Postmortem"
Irreantum: "Advice to a Young Mormon Poet," "Big City Prophet," "Daughter of the Pioneers," "The Great Mystery; or Isabelle Berry on the Eve of Her Demise,"

"Joseph Standing's Gun," "Resurrection Prayer," and
"Third Witness"

The Sandy River Review: "View"

Tiger Leaping Review: "Instant"

The Under Review: "Running Through Cedar Pass at Sunrise"

Vita Poetica: "Holy Envy"

Waves of Words: "Christopher," "Flight," "Restlessness on
the Flight," "Saint Melor," and "Second Grief"

Wayfare: "At Cold Harbor," "Pioneer Ascension," and
"Proxies"

As always, I express my love and gratitude to Sarah
and the children: Connor, Emily, Ella, Lucy, and Jacob. You
never cease to inspire.

And, yes, I thank Poe, our intractable Malshi. He has
been the silent and not-so-silent witness to the many hours
I've spent writing and revising this book. If nothing else, he
deserves the poem I wrote about him.

Also available from
GREG KOFFORD BOOKS

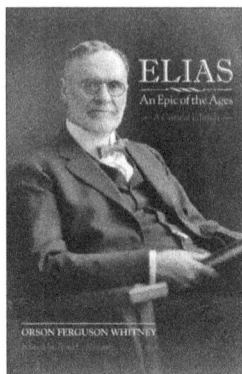

Elias—An Epic of the Ages: A Critical Edition

Orson Ferguson Whitney
edited by Reid L. Neilson

Paperback, ISBN: 978-1-58958-828-8

Orson F. Whitney's *Elias—An Epic of the Ages* stands as Mormonism's most ambitious literary achievement, a sweeping poetic retelling of the plan of salvation and the Restoration. First published in 1904 and refined in Whitney's 1914 edition, the ten-canto epic draws upon scripture, history, and inspired imagination to place the life and mission of Jesus Christ at the center of a cosmic narrative that spans premortality, the Savior's mortal ministry, the apostasy, and the dispensation of the fulness of times. In the tradition of Milton's *Paradise Lost* and Dante's *Divine Comedy*, Whitney sought to give his faith a literary monument equal to its spiritual grandeur—an epic in which doctrine, history, and prophecy meet in verse.

This new critical edition, edited by Reid L. Neilson, presents the definitive text of Whitney's 1914 revision alongside rich historical context, literary analysis, and contemporary responses that situate Elias in the cultural and religious landscape of turn-of-the-century Mormonism. Both a devotional masterpiece and a literary artifact, *Elias—An Epic of the Ages* invites modern readers to encounter Whitney's soaring vision anew.

Praise for *Elias—An Epic of the Ages*:

"Orson Whitney was the preeminent Latter-day Saint man of letters at the turn of the twentieth century. Reid Nielson has brought this ambitious writer and poet back to life with a critical edition of Whitney's vast poem *Elias—An Epic of the Ages*. Whitney sought to pour everything he knew and experienced as a gospel believer into one grand work. Neilson annotates *Elias* and embeds it in the sources emanating from Whitney's work: autobiographical reflections, contemporary reviews, Whitney's own critical work, and assessments of Whitney's overall achievement. Anyone interested in Latter-day Saint literature will want this book on their shelves." — Richard Lyman Bushman, author of *Joseph Smith: Rough Stone Rolling*

Imagining and Reimagining the Restoration

Robert A. Rees

Paperback, ISBN: 978-1-58958-828-8

In *Imagining and Reimagining the Restoration*, Robert A. Rees embarks on an imaginative and profound exploration of Latter-day Saint theology and culture. Through essays, poems, and midrashic interpretations, Rees sheds new light on foundational doctrines, the roles of prophetic imagination, and the divine narratives within the Restoration. He reexamines figures like Joseph Smith and Heavenly Mother, urging readers to embrace a creative and expansive faith perspective that transcends mere tradition.

This captivating work brings readers into a visionary discourse that emphasizes the power of imagination as a spiritual gift. With poetic interludes and scholarly insight, this volume is a transformative invitation to both imagine and reimagine faith, theology, and cultural belonging.

Praise for *Imagining and Reimagining the Restoration*:

"This is a beautiful book, a work of art. Enjoining us to imagine the gospel more deeply, it offers reflections on Christ, Mary, the First Vision, Heavenly Mother, and much else. Robert Rees wants to make us all gospel poets. He also seeks to make us religious critics. He gives his candid views of a broken church in need of mending, commenting on race, women's rights, sexual orientation, and earth stewardship with an imagination turned critical but still filled with warmth and good will. In the end, he invites us to imagine a kindly, loving church blessed with modern sensibilities." — Richard Lyman Bushman, author of *Joseph Smith: Rough Stone Rolling*

Dime Novel Mormons

Edited and Annotated by
Michael Austin and Ardis E. Parshall

Paperback, ISBN: 978-1-58958-566-9

Dime novels probably did more than any other kind of book to turn lower- and middle-class Americans into both book owners and book readers. They were so cheap that almost anyone could afford them, and so exciting that almost everybody wanted to read them. It's hard to tell just how many of these dime novels featured Mormons, but the way Mormons were portrayed in dime novels was remarkably consistent over many decades and multiple genres.

For this volume, four full-length dime novels have been chosen to represent different aspects of the Mormon image in dime novels:

- *Eagle Plume, the White Avenger. A Tale of the Mormon Trail* (1870)
- *The Doomed Dozen; or, Dolores, the Danite's Daughter* (1881)
- *Frank Merriwell Among the Mormons; or, The Lost Tribes of Israel* (1897)
- *The Bradys Among the Mormons; or, Secret Work in Salt Lake City* (1903).

The often-lurid and scandalous portrayals of Mormons in these dime novels had consequences for the relationship between Mormons and the rest of the United States. They would represent reality for millions of people, and the basic portrayals found their way into more serious literature. Understanding how these stereotypes were created and first employed can help us understand many things about the way that Mormonism has always functioned in American culture.

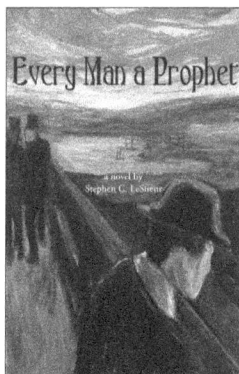

Every Man a Prophet

A Novel by
Stephen C. LeSueur

Paperback, ISBN: 978-1-58958-826-4

Every Man a Prophet by Stephen C. LeSueur is a powerful exploration of faith, love, and self-discovery set within the framework of missionary life in The Church of Jesus Christ of Latter-day Saints. Eddie Pedersen and Orrin Tanner, two missionaries serving in Norway, each grapple with the weight of expectation, personal desires, and the search for their true selves. Eddie struggles to reconcile his faith with feelings he has been taught to suppress, while Orrin's relentless pursuit of perfection masks a deep fear of failure. Together, they navigate a land of cold landscapes and colder hearts, striving to find meaning and connection in their spiritual calling.

Through Eddie and Orrin's intertwined journeys, LeSueur crafts a deeply human story of vulnerability and resilience. The novel delves into the complexities of identity, faith, and the universal longing to belong. As the two men confront the rigid doctrines of their religion and the unyielding truths of their own hearts, readers are drawn into an unforgettable narrative of courage and redemption. *Every Man a Prophet* is a profound tale of the sacrifices we make for faith and the truths we uncover about ourselves along the way..

Praise for *Every Man a Prophet*:

"In *Every Man a Prophet*, not only has Stephen C. LeSueur captured the lives, desires, trials, and struggles of young missionaries and their leaders better than in any other work I have encountered, **he has gifted the world with the best volume of Mormon fiction that I have read.** *Every Man a Prophet* touches hearts, opens minds, and changes lives. . . . It is a book that has the power to touch and change lives and maybe even wards, missions, and the Church." — Andrew Hamilton, Reviews Coordinator, Association for Mormon Letters

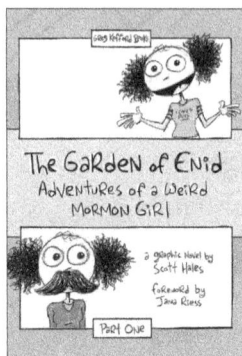

The Garden of Enid: Adventures of a Weird Mormon Girl

Scott Hales

Part One ISBN: 978-1-58958-562-1
Part Two ISBN: 978-1-58958-563-8

Fifteen-year-old Enid Gardner is a self-proclaimed "weird Mormon girl." When she isn't chatting with Joseph Smith or the Book of Abraham mummy, she's searching for herself between the spaces of doubt and belief. Along the way, she must grapple with her Mormon faith as it adapts to the twenty-first century. She also must confront the painful mysteries at the heart of her strained relationship with her ailing mother.

This edition of The Garden of Enid: Adventures of a Weird Mormon Girl recasts the award-winning webcomic as a two-part graphic novel. With revised and previously unpublished comics, it features the familiar story that captivated thousands online, yet offers new glimpses into Enid's year-long odyssey.

Praise for *The Garden of Enid*:

"Enid brings something real, something faith-affirming, something beyond Happy Valley and seminary videos and Saturday's warrior to the LDS audience." — Sarah Dunster, author of *Lightning Tree* and *Mile 21*

"This book is a classic whether you rush through it from cover to cover or linger over each moment, as the original readers did, at a pace of a few comics a week." — James Goldberg, author of *The Five Books of Jesus*

"Hales has created a world that will be an enduring addition to Mormon Literature. Don't miss this delightful work." — Steven L. Peck, author of *A Short Stay in Hell* and *The Scholar of Moab*

"There is much that Enid does not understand, just as there is much that I do not understand. But she makes me laugh, gives me hope for the future, and teaches me that it's okay to be myself: a weird Mormon girl." — Jana Riess, author of *Flunking Sainthood* and *The Twible*

www.ingramcontent.com/pod-product-compliance
Lightning Source LLC
Chambersburg PA
CBHW031542040426
42445CB00010B/669